SACRILEGE

BRENDAN CLEARY

Sacrilege

BLOODAXE BOOKS

ISBN: 1 85224 460 7

First published 1998 by
Bloodaxe Books Ltd,
P.O. Box 1SN,
Newcastle upon Tyne NE99 1SN.

Bloodaxe Books Ltd acknowledges
the financial assistance of Northern Arts.

Cover printing by J. Thomson Colour Printers Ltd, Glasgow.

Printed in Great Britain by
Cromwell Press Ltd, Trowbridge, Wiltshire.

For Curtis Mayfield

Acknowledgements

Some of these poems were published in Brendan Cleary's pamphlets *Goin' Down Slow* (Echo Room Press, 1997), *Sad Movies* (The Bay Press, 1996) and *White Logic* (Echo Room Press, 1996). The poems from *Radioland* were commissioned for performance on the *Mark Radcliffe Breakfast Show* on Radio One. The sequence *High Magic* was devised with music by Kathryn Tickell and Ric Taylor, and first broadcast on *Stanza* (BBC Radio 4). 'London Hearts' was published by Bernard Stone for Turret Books, London (April 1998, New Series, Broadsheet No.16.

Acknowledgements are also due to the editors of the following publications in which some of these poems first appeared: *The Big Spoon, Billy Liar, Dog, Get Rhythm, The Looking Glass, Melville's Dark Anus* (USA), *The Monkey Bin* and *The Wide Skirt*.

The author wishes to thank Northern Arts for a writing bursary in 1995 and the Society of Authors for a grant in 1995.

Grateful acknowledgement is also due to the following: Bernard and Mary Loughlin at the Tyrone Guthrie Centre, Annaghmakerrig, Co. Monaghan, Ireland; the Fine Arts Work Center, Provincetown, Mass., USA; the Royal Literary Fund; the Trent House Soul Bar (Newcastle upon Tyne).

Contents

SAD MOVIES

56   Chicken & Sex
57   Cloud
58   Dutch
59   Hearts
60   Hard
61   Mother
62   Prison
63   Suckers
64   Beverley
65   Airport
66   37
67   Sweet
68   Driftwood
69   Sally
70   Lily
71   Faye
72   Statement
73   Friend
74   1984
75   Secrets
76   Jam
77   Telescope
78   Family
79   George
80   Dream

THE NEW ROCK N ROLL

82   The New Rock n Roll
83   Art
84   Blind drunk
85   Boys' Own
86   Contacts
87   Marc
88   The enthusiast
89   Join Elvis
90   In the psychiatrist's chair
91   The soul doctor
92   Rory
93   London hearts
94   A man like Curtis
95   6 for Alison

GOIN' DOWN SLOW

Goin' down slow

I get strangely more deranged now
after 8 pints of Stella, pipes & spliffs,
was what the dissident student told me
over mushrooms & toast down at Luke's Diner
& I was confounded, terribly so!

What sort of Dr Frankenstein invented him,
yet looking so harmless in snow hat & anorak?
Let's take a closer look at his countenance!
Is that the sort of guy you'd rent a quarry to?
No way, Ray! He's shady, shady as the Holy Ghost.

So he gets strangely more deranged does he?
Big deal. That must make me the King of Sweden.
Are you on the make or all makeup? I ask him.
Are you sausages, eggs or bacon?

Philosophy, I rasped in his general direction,
Morality, Ethics, Theology, Logic or Physics?
You name your subject, professor. Luke, 2 beers!

By the end of the night we'd stumbled together.
I fell in the rain beneath a misty streetlight
& I told that dissident about crawling on the floor
looking for lost bits of Moroccan hashish.
I told that dissident student how I stare at your picture
& he just grinned & leered: *Yeah, Yeah, Yeah,*
same old story, squire, heard it all before...

Off stage

Katrina, why are holding that breadknife to his throat?
He was only trying to say he was really sorry, yet again.

It could have happened to a priest, well if priests took Speed
& priests tried to expose themselves to pizza waitresses.

It was only a practice run anyway, for some new production.
He likes to get inside the character's head. A lecher & creep,

that's what the spikey-haired director in braces told him.
So don't you see, Katrina, chasing Catherine up the back stairs

ranting *Come here wee girl, while I take a run at ye!*
was only his way of communing with his art, his master craft.

& that breadknife, Katrina, it does you no justice at all.
Best Sheffield steel, not even faintly blunted, are you drunk?

Think of the Assizes, Katrina, the jury all staring like storks.
Ignominy, Katrina, are you familiar with that concept, drop it!

Put it down in the name of Jesus, Mary, Joseph & all the saints.
He was only trying to say he was really sorry again, Katrina,

in the pub last night he swore on your beauty, he's a good bloke…

Planet Steve

I'm the only person living in the northern hemisphere
who doesn't know anyone at all, nobody called Steve.
Mark, John, Paul, Matthew, Tristen, Cecil & Marmaduke,
Sadie, Sally, Sue, Samantha, Priscilla & little Yogi
but none of my friends or acquaintances are Steve.
Nobody ever leans across to me on rush hour trains,
says *heard anything from old Steve this weather?*
or *where are you & Big Steve off to at the weekend?*
I spend my weekends going to drink & drugs parties
& in my wide experience no craze-faced gatecrashers
have ever come to the gate with bulging carry-outs
saying with pleading eyes *we're friends of Steve.*
Steve doesn't write me lonely letters from Southampton.
Steve doesn't leave enigmatic messages on my machine.
Steve doesn't ever pop by for a smoke in the afternoon.
In the afternoon the city clouds are pure & still
but Steve isn't here with me high, calmly contemplating.
He has never invited me out for the night to see *Hellraiser 3.*
He has never lent me a fiver till Giro day, not once.
& I know there are many famous people out there called Steve,
one plays snooker, one sings pop songs, with some conviction.
But how can I meet the famous, I use the same teabag for a week?
Meeting Steve will be like meeting a creature from another planet
Can anyone lend me a telescope to look for Planet Steve?...

Helen's boyfriend

& I think nice jacket captain, nice cloth,
pity about the utter fuckwit inside though
& he obviously has impressed her, obviously,
what with all that flicking about of her hair,
all that pretending not to understand, wide-eyed
& if she marries this eejit I'll disintegrate,
already in the middle of the night I sweat
& I go to the bog & feel I'm composed of dots,
no matter to speak of, I'm just dots darting
all over the shop & look at his tie, christ,
is he wearing that for a bet & she looks at me
& I look back longingly like a cocker spaniel
& she looks at him, his greasy bake & he leers
so I get up real polite, make tame excuses
with my head still intact, I phrased it later...

Unhappy Hour

So I asked her why she left,
it was because I am so ugly.

So I drink here at twice the price
with my desperate sad compatriots.

Him over there in the baseball cap,
that's Eric, his wife fell under a bus

& Big Arnold's mum has got cancer
& Rosie in the corner has lost it,

by 6 most nights speaking in tongues.
But these people are my friends

& they matter, drunk in slum basements,
stumbling heartbroken in the sticks.

We drink here at twice the price,
it's our own glorious sad republic.

People are my friends & they matter...

Giro Eve

£2.50 for my Best of Joe Tex again,
so it's milk & half an ounce of Golden Virginia

& imagine Panther, Redcar, 3.15, 11/1
racing inside my blue head if you can

then later journals, a girl in the library,
she has beautiful red hair & smiles

how could I dream of ever renting her
with just 43p in coppers, shrapnel,

hey fancy buying me a cup of coffee
lovely porcelain girl? wouldn't be cool

yet her face & eyes shine so majestically
with me getting closer to rolling butts,

me close to tears & crime, the slow clock ticking
& in the morning Dave Edmunds sings *Queen of Hearts*

on the ancient transistor beside my scratcher
& I cough & splutter with dust in my eyes,

rush like Rasputin would to my letter box,
watch that envelope in the slipstream, hit the mat

as if my time on the planet could begin again
as if when wished for all the stars could spin...

The death of Maria

There's this line from an old David Bowie album:
learning to live with somebody's depression.

That's me, I used to think on the sofa by the telly.
We'd sit there night after night amid the adverts

& usually I'd be daydreaming of escaping it all,
I even invented an imaginary lover in my head, Maria.

She was Italian, sophisticated, bisexual & best of all
everytime I walked into any room she'd swoon.

But then Maria kept fading when *Dynasty* was on
or *Family Fortunes* for a laugh, she receded slowly

until the day you waved the electric bill in my face
& Maria just about disintegrated. Bits of Maria

all over the kitchen, swallowed by our rituals. A shame.
A very deep hurtful shame, if the truth be known.

Long before I made Maria up I used to dream about you...

Britannia Hotel

I was promised hookers
strutting through the lobbies

I was promised the head
of John the Baptist on a plate

instead it's freezing & blood
is dripping onto the blanket

from where I cut myself now
just to see what would happen

& snow falls over Manchester
it's like a lonely graveyard

& the television is knackered
so Loudon Wainwright on my walkman

moans *come up to my motel room,*
save my life...

Paper women

It's raining, grime on the windows, so I think of her delights,
the beautiful woman with no excuses, all her chemical delights.

She straddles billboards, is all over smudged newsprint, bare,
everything laid out in front of me like a picnic in July.

The first sin always happens in a moment of weakness,
so Kierkegaard says, old Special K & look! Phantoms out there!

Street signals, bums in Levi's, slashed light & traffic flare
cut away the webs around my heart, it's frightening & my songs?

What of my songs? My songs are all of her, my paper queen,
the beautiful woman with no excuses, she wants my child.

In this dull coffee cup, roll-up zone of morning scum, I dream,
dream of sex up on the roof or in places that just disappear

& *Life has got too many corners to turn*, simple philosophy eh?
I keep looking for someone with no excuses to ease the pain,

probably the only lunatic around here who thinks he's not insane.

Soho Café

In Soho Café I found her
or so I thought

she wore black boots
& a tasteless poncho

had once been arrested
her conversation sexy

I even thought I'd kiss her
but she turned into her photo

the room smelled of beetroot
cups & saucers started dancing

so it was out to the rain with me
without my eyes I took the fear

& ran…

Shopping

At Safeways beside the veg
I have a blinding flash

you are making love now
with someone I'd recognise

I see your scattered books
the movement of your face

but everything must fade
as a woman like Lana Turner

picks up a beetroot jar
& the muzak has synchronised

with the fat man in a suit
carrying a giant box of Daz

until I see your eyes again
as a look of shock beckons

trembling at the bacon counter
until the next transmission

& it's raining like Monsoon
so I push my trolley slow

as if up the steepest hill
I push my trolley like a trooper

just trying to keep the faith...

Love in the nineties
(for Sarah)

don't shun it
or throw it away
it gets bad press
but it's precious

& I can remember
the shadows behind
your face & smile
even before we met

& it's true to say
every single day
I grin or raise up
a glass of porter

thank the chaos
for hurling you
in my way so much
in my direction

The Lads

After a feed of pints & a late-night smoking session
me & Big Greg needed a huge fry-up, then a cure.

At the corner table in Luckies we leered out at girls,
gave them marks out of 10 as they passed, bleary-eyed.

Greg reckoned his marriage was *up shit creek, completely*;
with no paddle, presumably, I added & he just grinned

as a beautiful blonde student girl glided by us, lithe,
gleaming in the sun that scorched our eyes inside.

I could see faint traces of tears in Greg's whirlpool eyes,
his wife had given a tough ultimatum, *it's the drink or me?*

Give up the bevy & the garden's rosey & many little bambinos,
the same old dilemma hurting, *an old war wound*, he called it.

Just about then I caught the glance of the barmaid daydreaming
as guzzling down his pint Greg gave 9 to a smart businesswoman,

she stepped from her taxi with the air of some film star
& Greg reckoned he loved *all that power-dressing lark.*

Fuck, he murmured, the sun exploding, our tongues hanging out...

Islands

Awkward silence has become our way of life
& you've been rattling your keys & pondering.

So I've switched on the TV to remind me I'm alive,
watching crowds at Southampton docks waving Union Jacks.

So this is it then? you mutter through gritted teeth,
while a mother of 3 weeps buckets on the screen.

Her man has lost control over himself, setting sail
to some vague landmark, people aren't sure where.

Listen! I lay claim to this house, this table, chair,
the entire LP collection, it's mine! Don't be bitter!

But before the first shell bursts on the runway,
before the tabloids yell *Gotcha*, you'll look up

defiantly as usual, as if to spit in my face...

Jealous guy

What do you mean why am I ringing at 4 in the bollox morning?
Yes, of course I'm drunk, listen, cheeky chops, can we try again?

Remember the Lake District, I can't forget the Lake District.
And Scotland & Sammy's Café & shagging in the squat afternoons?

& Welsh Jim says you're really still in love with me, admit it
& sure you had plenty of *Space* when Jim & I were at the match

& I never so much as looked at another woman, not even once
& there plenty I could have snogged, I deflected their glances,

I've made a lot of sacrifices, Welsh Jim says that's suffering,
he reckons those girls' faces will haunt me. There was Big Rosie,

wee Sharon, the girl at the fag counter in Littlewoods, at parties
there were heaps of them, begging for it, or so Jim reckons

& look I can't sleep & it's desperate, Chucky Bear, have pity
& I'm sorry for punching that hole in the wardrobe, honest

& I'm sorry for thumping the door, I'll fix the table promise
& I'm sorry for saying *I talk to you but you just don't listen,*

so you know me better than I know myself then. It was a mistake.

For Jim

hope the old tickers
don't give up on us, Jim,
you crazy epileptic

last week on the phone
your voice in slow motion
as if ciders & Specials
had got their grip again

hope the old ticker bears up
for all us obsessives, Jim,
for us dissidents, rocket-people

with my wife in the garden
in the leafy suburbs, Jim,
will my ticker give up then,
yours on a bus to meet a girl?

who will remember us, Jim?
our sad, weird & drunken
versions of the truth...

Dick

I'm sick of being lonely,
fucked-up, always stoned.

I knocked over the ashtray,
it was a ghastly omen.

It happened to Dick Diver
in *Tender Is the Night.*

He lost the plot, cracked,
began to think sadly aloud

every girl he saw he thought
I love you till I die.

So I drink here, an anti-hero,
a pissed-up parody of myself.

Drink is the heart's mercury,
I load it down my neck

as the jukebox blasts
that's me in the corner

losing my religion,
I space out at the bar,

think of lost companions,
their smiles & fears

& lovers with their faces alive...

E.

Last night in the bar
2 beautiful girls
spaced out on E
stood up on the stools
& did a sorta stripshow

we hung about like dogs
& my friend Dawn
also spaced out on E
said *Power, man,*
fuckin' great

I wanted to be unconscious

Afternoons on Jupiter

Typical!

as predicted
Steve weighed in
with his usual 1/2 gram

we spent the day
damp, in extremis

cartoons
wacky Brazilian soap
& I wanted beer
I always do

in the flush
of sunset I withdrew
stared, eyes on pins,
for could have been days,
at a piece of coloured glass
I found on my table
just lurking

Steve passed out
& the globe receded

as I twiddled...

The Grateful Dead

It's *The Book of Changes*
I told her
I'll show you later

Gram Parsons or
was it The Byrds
were rambling
& wailing as
I leant across

like steel guitar
her hair all gleamed
& she wore her beads
with a melancholy air

I thought of us
on some threshold
together smiling

I offered the smoke
to her birdlike hands
delicate & pale

I think there's a touch
on there, I grinned

& the songs all ended
& she giggled...

White logic

Last night everything slid
into perfect shape, crystalised.
After 4 bottles of Bulgarian
I rang you up around 2.23 a.m.
There was something I've always
wanted to tell you again, urgently.
Although distant, groggy with sleep,
I knew you'd understand.

Now in the thud of morning
my eyes sting, my head hurts.
I feel guilty about something
vague & totally indefinable.
Looking at the phone I wince
& remember snatches of my wild
drunken ramblings in the bar,
faces of the strangers straining
to hear why we had to fail.

Did you & I agree to meet
in the café this afternoon
to talk it all over again?
I hope to Christ we didn't,
that you think me a fool
& if we did agree on something
it was to forget. I hope so.

Last orders

My ex-wife with her cuddly dog
is with her lover's ex-mistress
who is talking seductively
to my brother's ex-girlfriend
& her partner now a lesbian too
who once had designs on me
before my boss's sister
left a message on my answerphone
saying my best mate's girl
really fancies me at least sometimes

It's all getting mighty confusing,
I thought
& I only popped in for a swift one
on the way over to my mum's...

Cross purposes

After discussing Marcel Proust
in the mayhem of the kitchen
with the girl in the tiny pink slip
I hear her tell the slim Anouska,
he's a really nice bloke him
he's like really really deep

but the girl in the psychedelic jumper
outside smoking by the fire escape
when I broached the same subject
turned & glared & called me
a total & utter prick...

Space

Go slow, she whispered, *it's not a race,*
but I was so excited I spilled my 4th beer.

She has the galaxy's most beautiful face,
my future without its shine is all fear.

Her leaving could make me into a basket case,
being so passionate is going to cost me dear.

She touched me & spoke, I didn't always hear,
then she said she wanted to have her *space*.

What? I moaned, bedraggled, *the final frontier?...*

A curable romantic

So what does it feel like then
sad dysfunctional romantic poet?

Well, I'll just be honest, if I may,
if that's excusable: pissin' in the wind

& something real & really beautiful's dying
so I'll grit my teeth on wet Tuesdays & bear it

& I have no intention of cutting off my ear
or dying consumptive on the steps of City Hall.

I'm just going to have to get real, whoopie!
After 17 years of that fuckin' bitch Thatcher,

her insidious legacy & that Paperman Blair
& the death of anything vaguely like a dream

of how it could be perfect, nothing is untainted
& if I'm honest it makes me want to explode

or blow up some national institution, why not?
It seems sort of natural to want to these days

at least when I stop & really think about it...

HIGH MAGIC

High Magic

1

a kiss for your
sad eyelids

a rainbow looms
above the bustle
of the city

reflections in oil
puddles & cold
sunshine in shadows

have faith
have no fear

2

we catch our breath
on park benches

crazy & stoned
look to the pylons
the shipyards

flecks of light
on the wharves
& radiance here
in city flowers

the sense of your
fingers' touch
suspended

3

outside in snow
the city trees
calmer than ever

in pale sun
twisted branches
spell your name

& I could wish
for older times
but why?

memories drip
into my heart
like mercury

& this is now
your skin so
perfect

4

Central Station
in the fast air
& tannoy blur

only 4 minutes
on the board
& a rush of blood

then spying each
dwindling carriage
to catch your eye

before sunlight
on platform 3
& I lift you up

swing you high
above myself
smiling

5

frost on our breathing
in miles & miles of air
speaks beautiful language
we translate in a bedroom
high above the terminus

squinting streetlights
from a towerblock bed
hands stroking hair

it's high magic

6

condensation scribbles
on the bedroom window

& soft fine rain over
the flyover's glare

I tumble to one side
of your hungry kiss

mesmerized by cars
chasing the dawn

like death itself

7 POEMS ABOUT HEAD

1

Standing in the shadows of love
blares out of the jukebox again.
Head watches the girl he thinks
is Korean. She sucks ice cream.
Some of the ice cream spills
on her blue silk blouse. A drop.
The girl Head thinks is Korean
fixes Head in her stare. Her
finger scoops up the ice cream
into her wide-open mouth. Head
remembers desire & walks out
of the café to the mad streets.
Her image stays in his eyes
as traffic swells about him
in the heat. At Leicester Sq
Head stops to roll a cigarette,
nearly fainting when he sees
her ghost again in all the windows.

2

Head daydreams on the escalator.
He is walking through the scrap
& Head is a child again, grinning.
Rows of rusting engines & bodies
of cars flash by his eyes in haze,
in the sun's vicious glare & Head
just wants to go back to before
the drugs took ahold & the fever.
In the scrapyard his father comes
from nowhere through a hole
in the clouds, at least Head thinks.
His father is calling *come home
Head, your mother has forgotten
your name*, his father shouts.
Head forgets the way he has to go,
the way he came & how to stop it,
the dreams & craziness that is.

3

Head wants to sleep for a decade
then crawl out of the trenches
in the spring, in the new dawn.
I'm floating & drifting high
over the rim of myself, he said
to the girl who poured him whiskey,
then said he was sad but so sweet.
The lights were on but there's
nobody in were Head's own words
when she came back to Head's place.
I have a hard time finding focus
for this kaleidoscope inside me,
the nightmares are burning me up.
She packed up her bits & split
calling Head a nutter which he is.
Head called after her in the wind,
you are stealing all my faculties.

4

Head spent the hour between midnight
& 1 on the phone to a sex kitten,
at least that's what the advert said.
She told Head what colour her pants were
& how she'd like to suck at him.
Head was unsteady from the whiskey
& it was hard to imagine her real
but Head tried his hardest, his hand
plunged down his underpants, his eyes
wishing the sex kitten were painted
on the wall, but with no emotions,
ready for Head to pounce, gracelessly.
Head hung up the phone that night
heavily depressed & he saw again
in the mist behind his skull, a dog
he held up for his birthday treat
in the snow garden with the swing,
as Head's mum crooned with joy.

5

Head is reminded of Crazy Josie,
she drank cider from his shoes,
she took him down to the river
where she later drowned on Speed.
The river's calmness soothed her
& the bottles of Vino Collapso
she drank there over the years
start to accumulate & multiply
in Head's sad version of events.
Crazy Josie once fell off a roof,
once slept upright in a phonebox.
She once wanked Head off down in
the tunnels of the new underpass.
He felt sick but she grinned:
That's what you need, Head,
a good going over, a seeing-to.
Rum laps around Head's stomach
& he burns for her cockney giggles.

6

Head feels so doggone empty,
there is no air in his head.
So he yearns for the promise
of trips to all the fleshpots.
Once in Soho, Head followed
a man on crutches, watched
as he climbed the doorway stairs
up to the room with HELGA.
Head rattled poor sad coins
as the man on crutches came
& Helga smoked & grinned a bit
thinking of her fix tonight.
She feels sorry for sad fuckers
like Head, lost in the peepshows,
an archaeologist of skinflicks.
Helga calls them fuckwits.
That's Head & the cripple both
stumbling out to the glare & drizzle.

7

Head takes a walk on the dark side.
There are demons sneering in the trees,
in the bushes his fears take the shape
of wide-eyed birds who stare & bleat.
Head gasps & moans & nearly chokes
when he thinks of his room he cries
all the extracts from Head's diary
are scattered on the floor & the bed
he lies wanking on in the still light,
until it's time for the rituals again
& the crazy gang arrive for joints,
talk astrology until the dawn
bleaches their faces & the Speed
makes Head feel like he has Mumps,
Scarlet Fever, but a pint helps,
or in his clearer moments Head thinks
of a pear tree in a garden in his past
dripping with beads of soft rain.

RADIOLAND

Poems commissioned for performance on
Mark Radcliffe Breakfast Show, Radio 1

Oysters

Naomi, Cindy, Claudia & little waif Kate
& every would-be Supermodel out in Radioland,

put down those hair-tongs, that lipstick, quick,
leave those eyelashes alone for just 30 seconds.

Listen to me, what a sexy sexy voice I have,
so how come we've never eaten oysters together?

& I've whispered your names, a litany to my phone,
I've saved all your snapshots from *Hello* magazine.

But you never call or write, you never fax me,
how come? Oysters, you & me OK, oysters & then, well...

Disclosure

I have disclosed my P.I.N. number again,
it just keeps cropping up in conversations.

Even at the grim-faced checkout counter I said
Thank you Ms Smith, I presume, 8470.

She looked up aghast as did the waitress,
Garlic bread twice please, 8470.

I just can't quit it, I must love thieves,
I must want renegades to steal my stash.

I break up discussions of Art & Literature,
I even bring the weather around to it, my P.I.N.

Guess I'm really bored unless everybody listens to me...

Sophie's Choice

Sophie from the stars page said I'd be poor,
that matters of the heart would rankle bad today.

So here amid the faces on the mall, on escalators,
I'm looking for all my new chums, the Gemini's.

$1/12$ of the population knows what it feels like,
if only I could meet them conveniently for muffins!

So that man with the squint & holes in his jeans
hoking through the bins this morning in Leazes Park

was clearly a Gemini too & to be sure, rest assured,
the sultry girl on the Metro with her head in a book

How to mend a broken heart quick by Dr Cheerful M.A.,
she was one too, I'd bet my hat, but we never spoke.

& it worries me Sophie could be wrong, her charts, who knows?
Burglars could have altered all her charts, who knows?

& Sophie was very vague when I wrote to her last month.
Any tips for the National, Soph, even the 2.30 at Ayr?

Later out of the blue, Samaritans rang, as if psychic themselves.

The Big Issue

What's it to be on toast in the calm sunlit kitchen
as cars below idly honk horns, honey or marmalade?

Some say, on their country estates or in their slums,
there are only 2 sorts of people in all this life:

Marmalade people & Honey folk, but I dispute that stance!
I'd like to sit on the fence again, not like my friends.

Alice, in her beret, once pushed honey through my letter box,
as if transfixed, Sam waxed lyrical all night about Golden Shred.

I wish I could be so decisive, then I'd always be invited.
Instead in my yellow sunlit kitchen I ponder the facts,

one man's honey is another man's marmalade, can I spread both?

Cake

Well if it's got marzipan on, then I don't care,
I don't want to have it or eat it, so it depends,

it all boils down to what's on offer, doesn't it?
Chocolate fudge with you in the bustle of the city,

coffee or caramel in the heady cafés of Amsterdam.
At least specify, I need to know where I stand,

on the cake question that is, it's not difficult surely?
At least give me a hint when our eyes next collide,

at least let me sneak a glimpse at the menu...

Small Victories

So they've started work on the bypass then, so what?
At least I was there in my combats & woolly hat,

at least my dog bit the foreman more than once,
I used to imagine the surgeons at his bed looking grave,

inspecting the wounds, no I did my bit & Kate says
she still wants to be friends, that's a partial success.

But best of all is the great vanilla yoghurt coup,
they took it off stock at Safeways but I fought,

a 37-page plea from the heart, I needed my breakfast,
no other flavour would do, manning the barricades,

trying to keep the vicious Fido on his string,
trying to keep Kate impressed, almost endlessly...

Heavy

& so at the soft drinks machine in Jim's Gym, sweating,
I remember how we kissed on the hard shoulder of the M62.

All the crazy traffic hooted & though we were windswept
beyond all reasonable degree, we just kept on kissing.

We had to do something until the obliging AA man came,
but even then we didn't stop, he dropped his sandwich shocked.

Kisses sublime & irrefutable, kisses hard to resist
& even when Jim's shuts, on the bus on the flyover home,

I'll still think how fine & healthy kissing you was,
the motorists waving their hankies, cheering our marathon snog.

But when I told Jim about this he frowned deeply,
he reckoned I should put in an extra few hours on the weights...

A Nature Poem

I mean how, how does it all work then,
tell me, you're the David Attenborough type.

A caterpillar becomes a butterfly, imagine it,
one minute crawling about in rain-sodden leaves,

the next flying above it all, beauty with a swagger.
I mean butterflies look nothing like caterpillars!

& as for us humans, what if we turned into trees!
Growing our hair for branches, saying *when I'm a tree*.

People would be afraid, I've found they are of change,
but turning into a tree is scarey, so it's natural.

Lord keep me away from factory clocks & full-length mirrors!...

SAD MOVIES

Chicken & Sex

Chicken & Sex. That's what I need constantly. I am quite insistent upon this but as usual she ignores me. Sometimes in the stillness, in the flakes of snow or leaves falling, sometimes it feels as if she is the one with all the problems & I am the therapist. It's costing me £20 to feel so special.

What's happening now behind her eyes? I've just been revealing to her what I truly need & crave. Chicken & Sex. She just gazes at the flakes of snow or leaves falling outside in the stillness.

Does all this therapy mean my entire childhood happened in some sort of warzone? Answers, I want them! Once she asked me what colour I would paint the world. That really stumped me. I made one up. A bright shocking yellow. Something that would distort all of our heads. Then she told me I masturbated too often. How could she have known that? She may be silent but she's wise.

One day when the flakes of snow or leaves weren't falling I arrived early, let myself into her studio. She had left me a virtually illegible note. I think it read: *Gone to see my therapist*. So she had one too, I was reassured. I noticed when she did appear she looked pale & her clothes didn't seem to fit. I know what that feels like. At that stage I had yet to mention anything at all about the Chicken & Sex. Those were happier days, less confusing. Now she tells me again over the decaffeinated coffee that I'm *getting there*. I still don't know what she means...

Cloud

Sometimes the clouds are my friends. I'm serious, I look up at the clouds & they seem to be smiling. *Wish I could put a piece of one of them in my pocket & take it out at really opportune moments, I used to say.* Cathie grew excited when I talked like this.

Sometimes in the clouds you can see big furry animals, I once told her. She accused me of taking drugs, which was outrageous. I knew a guy once who used to snort all sorts of stuff. He ended up in prison. My sister used to visit him because she thought she might be pregnant. He was a serious junkie. I just like a bit of tack. Not like Cathie. Once she swallowed 4 tabs of acid & it sent her mad. She's never truly recovered.

I remind her about the clouds. The clouds have come back into our lives again, majestically. Cathie has just gone to the car for a bucket of chilled wine. It's summer. I fumble in my pocket of my trunks where there is a tiny ball of cotton wool...

Dutch

It was an inspired idea, don't you think, to have eloped like this after a crazy night of whiskey drinking & made straight for Amsterdam. Now we are in the Free World Coffee Shop & I've just started another bizarre conversation about ghosts. I smoke the skunk grass & catch the eyes of the bald man at the next table who is listening & watching us fall deeper into the well of love. He is jealous of the light within our eyes.

By now all the folks back home in Ireland will have discovered us missing. They will be traipsing around checking all the rooms. They must suspect we are together but, don't worry, they will never guess we have come to ground here. I gave the taxi driver a hefty tip to keep silent should they ask. The flight was eventful because we kissed a lot.

I want to see a real ghost. One that looks like a swirling sheet, one that wails. A friendly ghost from a comic book. You tell me again I drive you mad with all this crazed fantasy stuff but you would miss it dearly if if I were dead. The bald man at the next table is close to tears. I reach over & stroke your smooth beautiful cheek. I wish love would find him here & he could share in its magnificent joys & visions.

Don't worry, my precious, they will never catch us up...

Hearts

On Valentine's night in *A Passage to India* they had tied heart-shaped balloons on the backs of all the seats. We sank about 6 lagers & then, well over the edge of midnight, wandered back up the hill in the Tyneside mist. Each time we kissed I felt a new blossom within myself.

We giggled our way up the hill with a heart each on a piece of string. Our hearts, in the raw mist, tried to flee from us with each gust of wind. I bounced my balloon against yours & joked about breaking your heart. I tied my balloon to my arm & joked about my heart being on my sleeve. The light rain came & fell & I remember seeing a few drops of it gleam for an instant on the frizzle of your hair as your eyes shone in laughter.

Eventually, in your bedroom, we let go of the strings. I felt pure & uncomplicated. The helium hearts drifted slowly up to the ceiling. We lay touching each other until we disappeared completely with a smile to break the past & lift the Tyneside mist...

Hard

When you're in love with a beautiful woman IT'S HARD. Dr Hook are blaring in my ear & surprise surprise I'm on my 8th pint. The 8th is the one that truly matters. The edge of the abyss. 8th grade.

Everybody talks to me these days as if I lived in a bubble. I feel as if I'm not supplying people with subtitles when I try to tell them exactly what I think. My life has been dubbed into an ancient dead language. Hardly anyone speaks it.

When you're in love with a beautiful woman watch your friends. Mine's just bought me my 9th. Last year he said: *She's beautiful, but I don't fancy her myself.* Now it's this year. I want my 10th. It's hard...

Mother

The passageway leads down past the room with the locked door. As a child I used to pretend that inside were the sort of secrets people would plot murder for. Eventually Joan let me look within. She knew my father would punish her severely. He had done so before, she claimed, spanking her with a cane. But Joan could tell how much I yearned to visit this secret chamber. She died last May. My father wore dark glasses at her graveside.

In the corner there were racks of old wine bottles. Dust in the air was so thick I coughed loudly when Joan let me in. *This is where your mother took all of her lovers*, she whispered. When she said that word, *lovers*, her eyes flickered. I sensed, even at such an early age, that desire was all around me & always would be. Now that I've grown up & had experiences I still think of the expression on Joan's face & the expression on my mother's face in the faded photograph I found on the mantelpiece. I was forbidden to mention her for many years, my father standing over me forcing me to count & spell when I wanted to run wildly through the fields.

The passageway leads to the end of all my dreams. Now Joan is dust. My father was eventually discovered & all of his depravity revealed to the world. The authorities came & took him away & took away his whips & clips. I felt great relief. Now in the mornings I wake & watch the sun glinting on my mother's face in the photograph with its dark erotic stare...

Prison

People who escape from prison get captured again because they think too much about where they've come from & don't think enough about where they're going. There's wisdom, I told her, pouring Jameson's whiskey into the glass in her bathroom where she kept her toothpaste & stuff. She lay in the bath humming with her thoughts in the bubbles. I noticed the first sprouting of an ugly mould on the wall. Nothing around here ever gets cleaned or decorated. I lost my sock in her bedroom once. It took 2 months to find it.

She is impressed with my theory. Who wouldn't be? It's deep. Profound. She stands up in the bath, some bubbles still clinging briefly to her stomach & thighs. She reckons my theory is a clever metaphor for *loads of things, loads of situations in life*. I've begun to wonder. Part of me means it all literally. That worries me. It's nearly dawn. There is no more whiskey.

Suckers

Your history, of course, was up for grabs. Sure, didn't you tell the whole tableful of drinks about the time you fucked your old boyfriend's worst enemy? Your old boyfriend kept ringing every 5 minutes as you lay back on the cushions in this guy's flat, smoking a Benson & Hedges as he grunted on top. *I had to do something to ease the boredom,* you said, then grinned. *He looked so pathetic.*

Then there was some other sucker who offered you the whole marriage trip. You told the whole tableful of drinks you only ever hung about with him because you loved his cats. Then there was the punter who split your head open, banged it on the floor. Then there was the anti-depressants. Then came all the Therapy shite you babble. Then me.

So I still try to imagine a weak pale sunlight on your face, straining through my knackered cane blinds, as you searched, possessed through all of my letters. Did the psychic tell you to do that too, I once asked you later, but you stormed off in a huff.

I reckon now it's my time to blab. I'll tell the whole tableful of drinks. Even the night we fucked in the bathroom in The Royal Station Hotel is going to be exhumed. I will divulge all the details to anyone who stands me a pint or Blackbush. Thank Christ you are beginning to fade away forever with all the memories that are not faintly beautiful...

Beverley

A teabag upon each of my stinging eyes, I lay flat out on the bed in an hotel room somewhere in West Yorkshire on an overcast Saturday afternoon. Myself & the beautiful ex-model, Beverley, had checked-in the night before. In an Indian restaurant she'd asked if I wanted to go dancing in Barnsley later. *What a concept!* I thought. When the bill came I scooped up a handful of coins & placed them next to her plate. O.K., she was a millionaire, but I wanted to contribute. I told her I would rather go somewhere & make love as strangers, so we did.

She went out for a drive through the hills in her sportscar when I was too weak & sick for sex. Memories of my ex-wife kept flashing through my throbbing head as I squeezed each teabag in turn, praying the 4 codeine I dropped & the joint would ease the pain. Beverley said when she got frustrated she drove her sportscar at 120mph. The adrenalin rush she got was somewhere near the thrill of sex, she insisted.

Before she returned, amid images of my ex-wife, I remembered the night before. Being so pissed, we locked ourselves out of the room. One of the porters had to let us in. I'll never forget the look on his face as we thanked him. Utter contempt. Lady & the Tramp. She was wearing all that classy sexy gear too, the whole shooting gallery. Black stockings & high heels she insisted on keeping on. She told me all about her career as a model in Japan & other places, & how she & her husband used to take copies of *Penthouse* to bed. I'd known her 26 hours before I knew she had children.

Eventually I removed the teabags & rolled about on the bed with her. We were like maniacs. A month later she wrote & said I now had a brief cameo role in her unpublished novel. I was too afraid of some dark feeling inside to reply or ever see her again. But I still look on the shelves for her "bodice ripper" when I'm listless at stations or at airports...

Airport

I went out to the airport, very hungover & tired,to meet you. It had been arranged for weeks, though you later told me how much you dreaded the idea I'd be there. I had misgivings as well, for what it's worth. Your father had driven out there to carry home your bags. He would sail over the rim of the horizon if you asked him. He & I made polite smalltalk.I suggested we give an award to the holidaymaker with the most ridiculous hat. There were more than enough to choose from. Your father's eyes darted among the crowd. I felt nervous & resigned. There was a gnawing pain in my stomach. I've felt it there since.

You were the last to walk out into the brightness on the other side of the gate. I saw you notice me but pretend not to. Then I watched you compose your tanned, freckled face. Your hair looked more blonde than I could ever remember. You said you hadn't slept for 36 hours. Whenever the strain of our supposed love grew too awkward you often suddenly complained of feeling terrible.

On the concourse in the noise & chaos you told me in Turkey you'd *thought things out*. I asked if you'd met someone else. *Not really,* you replied. I instantly knew what you truly meant. *I love you as a companion.*

But not as a lover? I asked. You dipped your eyes & half-whispered, *No*. I kissed you quickly & walked away without looking back. I took a bus home alone to my flat. Later, on my answerphone, you were crying & saying how sorry you were things had turned out like this. Secretly I was glad. I wanted you off my case. As your voice on the message grew even sadder I remember gulping at a bottle of Carlsberg I'd bought in & muttering *What a load of crap...*

37

For years she thought he had no living-room furniture. She'd never, upon 37 visits to his apartment, even caught a glimpse of the living-room's interior. It was a mystery. She would never comment upon his style or taste because she never entered. It was always, without fail, a case of his hand down her knickers in the passageway. They just didn't have time for discussion of lampshades or his choice of Expressionist prints if he had any.

Ah, the slow relentless passage of the seasons! 37 times, 37 orgasms on the hall mat. Rain falling on the porch used to frighten her witless. She used to imagine his other woman when it rained. There was no rational explanation. There seldom is. It scared her witless anytime, the thought of his other woman, but especially when it rained.

One day it will have to end, she mused. They were lying in the hall, her tights askew, his boxer shorts clinging to his ankles making him look stupid. His unopened bills were scattered about. Once she had to step over a toy tractor his son had lost. She squirmed. *One day it will have to end...*

Sweet

That was Klaus, the waiter you told me about, on the phone, darling. He wants you to ring him back in Berlin. He seemed very keen. Look, this might not be the ideal time, but was there something going on there, darling? was what I said to her when she came in all flustered, overladen with shopping. Clattering down a 2-litre container of milk on the sideboard, she looked up at me in shock. *Klaus, Klaus,* she kept repeating & if I could have seen inside her head, I thought, there would be panic buttons flashing. If the inside of her head were electrical circuits she'd be in danger of a nasty wee explosion.

Of course it all turned out pretty grim. Klaus & her did. They did. They did have a snog on the dancefloor to Roxy Music's *Avalon.* She thinks it was *Avalon,* but anyway it was some smoochie number. *It was a snog, just a snog.* Emptying out the cans of beans from her basket she paused & looked at me real meaningfully. *It was just a snog. But you wanted to?* I gasped. *Yes, I did. Yes I did. I did want to!* she snapped.

The whole thing blew over, at least on the surface. Little did she know that for days & days I set the pause button on that image swimming around my eyes. Her & Klaus. Their tongues. Recalling Muriel last Christmas, in the back of her car, I resolved there & then we'd put it both behind us. I got up to make us both a cup of tea, with plenty of sugar…

Driftwood

This is the perfect dream of mutual consent. Although your name is Karen, you want me to call you Kim. Fair enough, Karen, I can handle that. But tie the knots a bit tighter, please. That blindfold is pure Marks & Spencers' silk.

So Karen, sorry Kim, what's it to be? Whiskey or whiskey with water? The bedroom or the bathroom or right here in the kitchen where an old soup tin has just rolled from the binliner & the whole place stinks of yesterday's aubergine curry? Backwards? Forwards? Upside down, Kim? & if I seem a bit distant it's only because of the drugs, OK? It's only the drugs have made me like this, Kim...

Sally

At Grassy's party, locked in the bathroom, I asked to see your breasts. Standing, staring at me, in the dry bath you took your top off. When I stooped towards your nipple I can remember thinking *beautiful!* but everything was really a drunken whirl.

Our laughter felt as strange as the look in our eyes when we sneaked a glimpse when kissing. Then Mark & all his mates started hammering at the door. *I'm bursting, for Christ's sake!* he kept bleating. I felt vaguely excited at the idea of being caught red-handed like that.

I walked you home past the graveyard in the nearly-dawn. Because you were locked out of your parents' bourgeois home with all its magazine racks & Penguin Classics & furniture straight from the Sunday supplements, I agreed to give you a foot-up over the back wall. When for a split second your very delicate foot balanced on my head, we both giggled. We were very high.

However the next day when I called you said you had a boyfriend & Grassy told me in her kitchen, smoking a hangover joint, you had taken cold feet anyway, a severe case of it. So I never saw you again. I certainly didn't call into that designer shop you worked in just off Regent street when Grass & I were in *the smoke.* I had a huge boil on my nose at the time, I felt really crap.

So Qué Sera Sera, Sally, I think. Maybe it's true we've both had 10001 drunken snogs at parties since.Whatever they are supposed to mean or explain, whatever they are supposed to signify?...

Lily

He sure was a real strange guy that Head Gardener. Sat there in his Tibetan skull cap, surrounded by old pin-ups in that littered office. Foliage seemed to be sprouting from the ceiling. Weird stalks & heads of flowers hanging everywhere so haphazardly.

I'd come such a long way to buy for you a single lily. Don't ask me why? That Head Gardener didn't even look up from his puzzle book, when I first appeared, tapping so tentatively at the door.

Hey, whatcha know? What can I do you for then? he spat in my direction. *Just a single lily for my sweetheart,* I replied & caught the faraway gaze of Miss October behind him on the wall. She was topless & holding up a giant beachball. I think I'd travelled all this way, along all those back roads, to take my mind off the kind of gaze that girl was giving out. I knew the Head Gardener could sense my unease. He spat a thick globule of phlegm into the litter bin. *Lilies, Sure I've got lilies, you like to tell me something about this true love then? Vital Statistics? Get my drift, little brother?*

I just didn't know what to say. I couldn't wait to leave that Head Gardener's lair, petals from all his flowers dripping everywhere, his spit, Miss October & that gaze. The single lily he'd wrapped in cellophane fell off the dashboard once or twice. Then near the turn-off to your place, I can't explain why, I threw it out the window. I watched the breeze carry your lily far off into the dusk, into all the time we'll never get to spend with one another, not ever again...

Faye

Years before we met, darling, the woman who looked like Faye Dunaway came into my life. Leeds station, 1989, I recall. I trailed my rucksack full of toys into the buffet, slumped down in the corner seat, smoked 3 Marlboro in a row & then rose to the bar for a double Bacardi, which for some reason was on special offer.

When I returned the woman who looked like Faye Dunnaway was sitting there, as if waiting for me. *I'll tell you who you look like, Faye Dunaway, the actress*, I told her. *Everybody tells me that. Would you like to come back to my flat? Why are you carrying a rucksack full of toys?* she replied. *So are you an actress then?...No, I'm a drugs dealer.* The whole episode over the years has somehow got fuzzier.

The woman who looked like Faye Dunaway's flat was a total mess. Bin bags stacked up, a used syringe on her bedside table next to some books about keeping a window box. Mind you, she had no such thing as the windows were all frosted over & didn't look as if they'd be opened for years. She was a strange fish.

The more I looked at her the more she looked like Faye Dunaway. It occured to me that maybe back in the buffet she had spiked my drink, that she was really hatching some sort of plan to steal my rucksack full of toys. Anyway, I told her I needed to use the bathroom. It was filthy. Shit encrusted on the toilet bowl, no bog-roll, just scraps of torn-up newspaper in an untidy pile. She kept a half bottle of Vodka where most folk place their toothpaste & brush. I made up my mind to escape.

When I re-entered her bedroom the woman who looked like Faye Dunaway had disappeared. I snatched up my rucksack full of toys & ran in desperation back to the station. My train for Manchester left at 3.25. I paced the platform, very anxious for its arrival. *Christ, let me out of this place!* I kept repeating & my legs felt like jelly & I was shaking...

Statement

Children, I'll just take a raincheck, if that's OK with you? But there's no need to go sulking up in your bedrooms, no need to have a tantrum when I refuse to get you ice cream, jumping up & down on the spot squealing *it's not fair! it's not fair!* It isn't.

Masters of war, you've sprung the worse fear that can ever be hurled, fear to bring children into the world. Bob Dylan said that & I've never argued with him. Anyway, what would be the point of me procreating, bringing a load of you lot to the whole gig?

One day when one of you was whining, feeling all broody & dejected after only getting a D grade or after missing a complete sitter from about 3 yards out, what would be the point in me being around to offer comfort. There is none. It's all grim & then it gets grimmer & then it gets even grimmer still & you die. I couldn't bare that sort of strain, Why should I?

So, all you unborn ones, as far as I'm concerned you should stay that way. I'm not cleaning up after you lot! & no I don't want to help you with your maths & I don't want to play rounders. & then you'd grow up! Fuck sticks! One day I'd be relaxing on the verandah, being all wise & learned & literary & you'd weigh in with some new partner. Someone ugly. Someone with spots! & I'd have to pretend I liked them & make ridiculous smalltalk about rain or salad bowls or pop groups with stupid names. The strain, I just couldn't bear it. I'd be a basket case. So listen don't be getting any ideas, stay away from my front door, the lot of you.

Friend

'It's a question of staying friends with yourself'. Why had nobody told me that before. I could have done with hearing that sort of talk every night as I get wrecked. Weed. Wine. Beer. Jamesons. Duty-Free Vodka. Anything. & when I think of the girls I tried to snog! In my more reflective moments I think sometimes that really I'm a bit of a sad little fuck.

Then you come along. I feel sort of clean all of a sudden. It's magic. I like this. I like being friends with myself. Thank you. I'm an all right guy. I like this feeling so much I think I'll sleep with myself tonight. Think I'll take myself out to the pictures. I wonder will myself like Jack Di Niro.

Seriously, what you said that night in the Bacchus Tavern has really made a difference. Gail had been giving me a load of grief. You remember Gail, how I called her *Looney-Tunes*? She thought I wanted to shag loads of young women. *Simultaneously, if it were possible!* I remember thinking, but I didn't let on.

Then you come along & your favourite things are perfume & champagne. That's cool. With your Philosophy degree & all that wild hair & all the beauty in your mad soul, you come along. *Well*, you said, *young women are very beautiful & you're an attractive man, what's your fucking problem?* What a relief! It seems I'm normal after all...

1984

I just knew when I got in the car this guy was a basket case. Soup Sandwich! He was smoking a menthol cigarette for a start, but it was the Oxfam suit & trainers combination that confirmed it for me. The lift didn't reach the top floor. Soup in a basket! Need I convince you more?

It was somewhere in Yorkshire on the A1. I'd stood there, smoking & kicking dirt, for maybe 40 minutes when along came this candidate. He didn't even look at me, the way folk check you out. He just pulled up & ushered me in, any hitcher would do. It was nothing at all to do with my natural charisma.

He reckoned he worked for his uncle's solicitors firm. He'd helped himself to 25 quid of the petty cash & got caught red-handed. His uncle's partner, let's call him Eric, was always stalking the office, on the lookout you might say. Eric wanted retribution, *Go & get punished, someone has to cane you & I won't tell uncle Henry.* Some script, eh? Truth stranger than fiction & all that.

Just near Doncaster he popped the question. I knew it was coming. Both his feet in those dodgey trainers were twitching. *It occurs to me, perhaps you could help,* he blurted. *Sorry, Captain, I can't oblige, can you let me out at this roundabout,* was my curt reply. Was that harsh, inconsiderate of me?

The next roundabout was occupied by about 60 Police. Loads of meat wagons. They were trying to break the miners' strike. A few days before some miners hurled a concrete brick off the motorway bridges, I think someone got killed. *Here's the fuck you should be questioning,* I felt like yelling. The candidate, still desperately unpunished, turned & sped back the way he came. Doubtless he gives his script to any poor hitcher just trying to see his mates or girlfriend down in *the smoke...*

Secrets

Around 3 in the morning the door swung ajar. I'd be reading about Harry Houdini, his bizarre obsession with lunatic asylums. You were slumbering in that old armchair my Aunt Marie left me. I don't like to mention it, but you had dribbled a little. Spittle all down your favourite sweater. I was just about to wipe it when the door started to play tricks. Next thing I know the bread just fell off the sideboard.

I remember shaking you, *Bert, wake up, we've got a visitor. Bert, someone from the Other Side has come to check us out, wake up!* My words were chosen foolishly. Next thing I know all the lights cut out & my throat started feeling real tight. I hadn't meant to be irreverent, honest, but this spectre, this presence, whatever it was had clearly taken offence. I'm often too flippant & some folks have said before it will get me in bother. Here was proof, Bert.

Surely this is just some weirdo dream I'm having, I thought. All this reading about Houdini, how he once walked right through a brick wall, or appeared to. That was long before Tony Curtis played him in the movie had been my reaction to this fact. Sure enough, even then I felt a strange twinge in my chest, a faint but discernible stabbing sensation.

By the time you woke all bleary-eyed, things had got back to normal somehow. The lights were on again, the door firmly shut, the bread back on the sideboard & the tension in my body eased. I must have passed out for a few seconds. I just remember a falling sensation, as if off a building maybe.

Don't ask me, Bert, why I'm telling you this all tonight. Up till now is all I've ever held back. I didn't know how to broach the subject. Please, Bert, put your arms around me! I hope I haven't spoilt everything. If I have, don't say, Bert. Let's muddle on like we have been doing. Let's pretend it's all OK, OK?...

Jam

It was such a wild party, although unlike Fatty Arbuckle's nobody got injured or killed. No extensive court hearings in the aftermath. No bribed witnesses, just bed for nearly a week for most of us. Champagne in the bath, mountains of Cocaine on the glass tables, sex in the hallway upside down. I couldn't read small print for a fortnight after the shenanigans we had. If there were awards for excess I reckoned I was due a Nobel Prize.

Now in the calm reflection brought on by the stillness of this slow July afternoon on the patio, you are asking me what the main highlight was. That's easy. It was the Anarchists stealing all the jam tarts. They lifted 14 platters of them & ran, a highly organised gang of master thieves. There was pineapple jam, gooseberry, blackberry, all types of flavours.

How those Anarchists cavorted in the swimming pool with all those jam tarts! They smeared jam on each other's faces, they threw handfuls of jam at each other in mock fights.They were all stuffing themselves with jam & rubbing it everywhere!

Around 3 Arnold was in despair. He was a stickler for decorum. *The flipping Anarchists have stolen all the flipping jam tarts*, he kept yelling, waving his arms about like a madman. Yes, that was definitely the highlight. Everything else pales into insignificance. Now tell me if you've ever witnessed a phenomenon quite like that? Bet you haven't, have you'?

Telescope

I imagine myself in Heaven looking into your bedroom through a huge telescope. You are lying leafing through *Delta of Venus*. We used to agree which passages were sexiest, which bits over-poetic & overwritten. I don't have a copy up here but I still remember all our conversations. Even being dead can't take your memory away.

Now you are sitting on the bed, rocking back & forth. It's how you meditate, you used to tell me. I always wanted to hug you when you told me you were in a phase like this. Don't suppose I'll get the chance now.

This telescope is clouding over! I need to adjust it. It must be the lens! No, there is someone there with you! Hey, this is getting out of control! We never did anything like that! This is pretty sexy stuff! Still, he seems a decent fellow. Watch out for him when he crosses the road & don't let him start taking class A drugs either. Learn from experience, if nothing else.

Now your bedroom is empty, *Delta of Venus* is open at page 43. If only this telescope were an updated model. If only it would focus. If only I could. This is a terrible place, my love! Not a day goes past without you in my thoughts, us making faces at each other & giggling like hyenas in each other's arms. But look after this new lad, he seems a worthy successor. At least that's what I reckon, confused as I am & hopelessly disempowered & disembodied...

Family

Confound your uncle, Verity, the vicious philistine tyrant! I'm the Great Raymondo & the Great Raymondo I'll stay, long after that pen pusher is poking the daisies up.

Yes, I take his point, but it will always depress me, Verity. It's a bitter pill to swallow. It will always fill me full of dread. Why can't we live on air? OK, some folk get up at the squeak of dawn, drag themselves onto trams for factory benches. Some people carry the weight of the centuries on their stooping shoulders & some people, Verity, like your uncle, just live in books, books & reports, the hypocrites!

What precious uncle Harry & his fat colleagues think when they're guzzling down the port in their club, holds little interest for me, Verity. But I'm no waster. & I can kiss as well as I can juggle. Tell the old crone that. Tell him to stick that in his pipe & smoke it!

I can flip 6 tennis rackets into the air & just keep them rolling. Some people think it's magic. They pour out of the taverns & I can eat fire! Can your uncle do that? Does your uncle understand velocity & rhythm? Can Harry inspire the masses with such sorcery?

Or is it because I often kiss you in the public square? Or is it because the word has got back that I can even juggle you & all your maids, tossing you all up in the air, catching you all with ease? So tell him, Verity, he can stick the dowry. The old scroat is only jealous. I'm the Great Raymondo & for better or for worse, Verity, the Great Raymondo I'll stay...

George

A fat bald man wearing fishnet stockings & high heels has just passed me by. He was carrying a transistor radio, clutching it to his ear like a seashell. I think it's too late, but I feel I should turn back & follow him. I think I can remember him from some dream, before they discharged me. George! That's it! His name is George. I can't remember where he lives but it's somewhere near here, I'm certain.

Nobody else seems to have noticed George. The group of Goth kids lying out on the grass smoking don't appear to have. Perhaps to them George is invisible. Look! One of the Goth kids has wrapped a snake around his midriff. He's sneering at that girl with purple lips. She's got a tattoo of a black crow on her cheek. *Hey, Joanne is in the happy box!* I hear him chanting this over & over again. Before they discharged me they told me people would say strange things & people would do strange things too.

Where did George go? Maybe George is in the happy box. That would explain it. Now my eyes are lighting up like bulbs. They did say this might happen. They did warn me...

Dream

I knew the heavy drinking had to stop when Doctor Diamond, in her sexy white coat, held up that photograph to the lamp for some serious scrutiny. My liver. It looked like some of the grimiest parts of Burnley on a November afternoon in a thunderstorm.

& then the jitters & shivers & shakes. When they all kicked-in I started to feel like a muppet. & then the insects, the crawling heebie-geebies. One day I just lay on the bed & watched them coming straight for me across the carpet. I had to throw the *Daily Telegraph* down & cover them up. *That's better*, I remember thinking.

Doctor Diamond is very sexy. It almost makes me feel grateful for being so sick. I get to see her twice a week. I'm hoping given time, which admittedly I don't have a lot of, given the right opportunity things between her & me might just develop. She already wants me to bring her my urine.

But all this drinking! She asked me when it all started. I just couldn't think. My head went blank. When exactly? At what age did I first neck a bottle of cold Becks? How many have I fired back since? Seeing that look in Doctor Diamond's eyes, I wish I had counted them all, every one...

THE NEW ROCK N ROLL

The New Rock n Roll

Still, there was quite a decent turn-out really,
at least 25 if you count Seamus, the organiser's dog.

Where were all those teenage girls in his sweatshirt,
his dressing room crammed with bottles of Jim Beam?

Traces of cocaine on a dog-eared limited edition,
rumours in tabloids he'd trashed his hotel room again?

& how come even though he dresses in all that black gear,
clearly the broody type, he can't whip us up to a frenzy?

Last night there was no crazy rocking in the aisles,
we weren't reciting along with him, swaying like geese

& we never held our lighters up, grinning near the end,
when he kicked into his sonnets like anthems...

Art

Tossing her blond curls about so haphazardly too,
tearing into the bites & nibbles as I approached.
This Derek, he's a conceptual artist, prizewinner.
Do you eat fresh sardines, then save the bones for him.
Derek's building a city for the Millennium this week,
he needs bones for roof slates, he'll paint them blue.
Art in all its many guises is no bother to this lad,
he once dressed up as Trotsky & went on the dodgems,
he once punctured the heart of a sheep with an ice-pick,
every third Tuesday he doesn't sleep or eat, a protest.

Her mouth agape & blubbering she fled into the kitchen
pleading *Gloria, get me out of this madhouse,* squealing,
they're all mad, flipping mad as spoons, Gloria, help!
But Gloria had slipped upstairs into Derek's studio,
poking about, utterly transfixed by the cow on wheels,
the pigeons smeared in molasses, the mechanical insects.
& Gloria looked more than just a little bit excited too,
by the time the pair of them scarpered, slamming doors.
Around then Derek & I were leaning back on the cushions,
raising our champagne aloft, both in fits of giggles...

Blind drunk

When the screen first went back
I thought you were lovely & sweet
but I know now you're a psychopath.

Cement is lovelier, or concrete,
yet I kissed you under a palm tree,
held your hand on a smoke-free jet.

& true number 2 had a cute little mouth,
I agreed number 3 plied on make-up,
but then you threw a toaster at me.

Round then the strain was really great,
so when you screamed I fancied Cilla
I just cracked. I called in the shrink...

Boys' Own

Sure Jo & I used to spend hours doin' it,
tinnies in the fridge & digging sounds like,
we'd think up ridiculous Country titles.

Remember Ireland's rugby team, a cracker
*Dropkick me, Jesus, through the goalposts
of Life*. It's a pretty hard act to follow.

& Jo always said politely: *Another beer there*,
it glided down smooth like a torchlit procession
as I kept a watchful eye on his whiskey bottle.

One night we just creased, ended up in stitches
when Jo came out with *Jesus stole my girlfriend*.
OK, maybe you had to be there, know what I mean?

Contacts

Susan, Sandra, I can't honestly remember,
but we weren't ideally suited for certain,
though her cheeky advert was appealing.

A seafood joint! Very fishy! That's right,
I can hear you gasp, oysters & prawn stuff!
Last time I eat paella I nearly suffocated

& I could just rot, turn into my furniture,
so why not seafood with an ugly sister then,
on her black suit a snowstorm of dandruff?

But she could drink, I give her that much,
Martini, I hear you gaffaw, but hang on there,
Vermouth's fine, at least after the first 11

& no we won't be dating again. That dandruff!
I kept thinking about Siberia. Fish soup & worse,
she smacked my hand for using too much salt...

Marc

Around '72 in Greig's café, Marc,
TK put *Jeepster* on the jukebox
& some wee girl I used to fancy
squealed *T Rex, who could beat em?*

Only a few years after that, Marc,
you wrapped your motor around a tree.
All the colours had been merging
& it's just been the bargain racks since.

Fuck! It could have been another story!
I know you'd have pulled a few tricks
out of your corkscrew hair by 1989,
I always imagined an album with Eno.

Then again, Marc, so much never happens.
I used to think everything had direction,
but suddenly the whole gig gets cancelled,
someone pulls out all of the plugs.

So I cry sometimes at the scratches
on the albums I chucked up in the attic.
Sometimes, Marc, I feel kind of cheated,
kind of sold short. I feel so beguiled.

The enthusiast

OK, this is goin' be my swansong,
set em up & I'll be knockin'em down,
Becks for breakfast again at Jim's

& if my days were pints of Guinness
I'd really want to live in them,
sometime I'd probably overdoze –

I wish my days were fingers of rum,
remember sinkin' them with Grassy
& the blues at The Broken Doll?

So let's get my system sorted out
once & for all, fill me to the brim,
pour it into my dangling legs & arms –

Slop it all over me, slop it quick!
Look this is my swansong & tomorrow
Becks for breakfast again at Jim's...

Join Elvis

Talk about Caligula or The Incredible Hulk,
he's even fatter than I could ever imagine

& in the afterlife too he's still obsessed
with fry-ups, King Burgers, peanut butter.

It was them Goddamn slimming pills did for me,
he confided & those last tragic days in Vegas,

remember him all bloated, slurring his lines,
forgetting huge chunks of *Lonesome Tonight?*

Well, he reckons it was then the curtain fell
& after that he just turned into a lookalike.

Spotted at a pancake house, a supermarket,
stalking the gardens of Graceland after dark.

So many sightings. Folks just can't accept it,
when whatever they believe in just vanishes.

But here's the twist, here's the big revelation,
don't quote me but it's true, he does go back,

even to the moon! He's not just fat but bored...

In the psychiatrist's chair

I've grown so docile recently, clumsy & ham-fisted,
my favourite dream is the one of being fast asleep

& regarding yesterday, I got stoned & missed it.
It's the excess of these party living rooms, the heap

of Skunk grass I keep by my bedside. Money! I pissed
it up against the scullery wall weeks ago. What was deep

is now shallow. All the meaningless shags I've listed
in a blue notebook I bought in Amsterdam. I keep

remembering afternoon cafés there, pretending I existed.
My friends say the road to recovery is long & steep

but when I'm not around call me bitter & twisted...

The soul doctor
(for John)

Christ on a BMX, Soul Doctor!
When I first saw all those albums
over in your gaff at Monkseaton

I just couldn't even start lookin',
it would do my head in completely.
Ancient Joe Tex, Gene Chandler Live,

loads of wicked 12-inchers too
straight from Kingston, Jamaica,
cornflakes packets for sleeves.

Aye, we're great men for our sounds,
that's why you keep spinning decks,
cart boxes of albums up 17 floors.

See, John, when a tragedy comes along
or just a strong blast of sunshine,
there's a tune for it. We understand.

Rory

As a man for the scooping myself,
your obituary & tributes, Rory,
put the fear of God into me.

So what's it like then being dead,
drinking in all those blues bars
up in the crazy side of heaven?

& you were a hero, that's a cert.
Comin' on with just the mandolin
meant you do *Goin' to my Hometown*.

That used to send me to the moon,
it made me feel like I'd bother
having any sort of future after all.

Aye, 4 or 5 pints, seriously under-aged
in Kelly's Cellars or The Washington,
Sean & I wired to the Black Mountain.

You were a sort of honorary prodigal son
at the Ulster Hall, the craic up to 90.
For years I'd still want your autograph,

like when I saw you up Charing Cross road,
slouching a bit in black with your guitar.
Rory's looking rough, I remember thinking...

London hearts

But yet we'll greet them with a kiss in the dirty light
at Embankment or under Soho with its broken promises;

or it could be in parks with flowers, on the tourist trails,
in the heat & grey of Piccadilly. Who knows, strangers?

So we'll just go on being strangers until something clicks
& it's time to go out dancing again. Work will grow easier,

phoning one another from offices or callboxes & on the tube
none of us will ever feel like an alien with our face contorted.

As from today I'm going to practise smiling more, smiling
& waiting. Then I'll make my vital London connection.

A man like Curtis

Keep well balanced & lean toward the sun,
but Curtis, don't you know, it's a hard old station,

most nights pissed or completely banjaxed,
most nights hearing your sweet charm in a haze.

& yet my heart tells me we're brothers, Curtis,
& *For Your Precious Love* & *Move On Up.*

Your endless smile from the soul & so much joy,
even paralysed from the neck down you grin

your wheelchair magic, your simple philosophy,
'Get on back to livin' again. Go for it Mayfield,

that's what Aretha says & who can argue with her?
Curtis, you make the sunshine come back quickly,

you make a kiss as it should be, irrefutable,
you're the president of my own world council.

A freak gust of wind, that lighting rig fell on you,
but 10 or so years on you can still breathe in love.

How many of us, Curtis, in our haze, can say the same?